Daisy the Dachshund's "Tail" of Recovery

By
Shannon King

© 2019 Shannon King
All Rights Reserved.

No part of this book may be reproduced, stored in a retrieval system, or transmitted by any means without the written permission of the author.

First Published by Daisy Mae Books 3/14/2019

ISBN: 9780578462813

DAISY MAE BOOKS
Bloomington, Indiana
www.daisymaebooks.com

Hi there!

I am Daisy the Dachshund! You can call me Daisy or Daisy Mae. I am 12-years-old. I live in the country with my brothers, Bundy and Handsome Hank, my best friend, Savannah and our mom, Shannon.

I have lots of stories to share with you; this one is my "Tail" of Recovery – I hope you enjoy it!

I have had a good and happy life in the country with my family. Most of the time my brothers and I behave.

We don't really do anything bad when we misbehave, although Hank has been known to bring a mouse into the house (interesting morning for Mom that day) and we have eaten things we are not supposed to.

We have no concept of time so when Mom is working it feels like forever. We entertain ourselves. There is a lot to do in the country! We have our own door to go inside and outside. This helps when we need to go potty (or Hank wants to bring in a mouse) and of course we have access to water all day.

Last summer, Mom came home from work and I was on the floor, unable to move. I was telling my paws to move, but they wouldn't. I remember feeling a little like this before (after I have eaten something I am not supposed too) but not quite this strange.

Mom picked me up and got on the phone. We went to see a vet in town. I could tell she was scared. I was scared too.

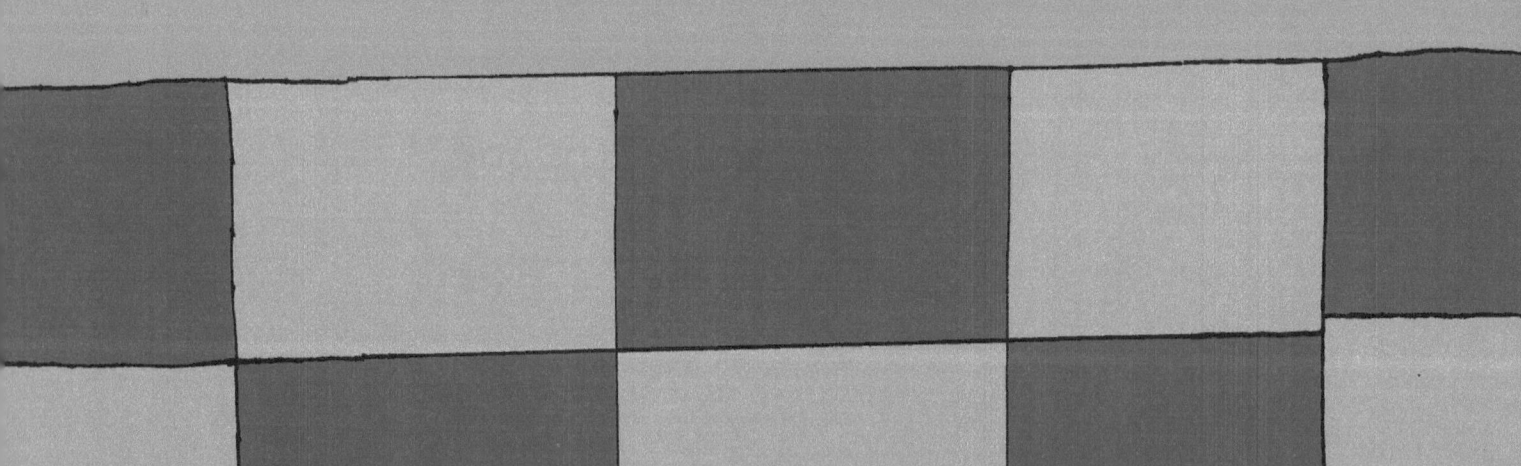

I heard the vet tell my mom that I could "go at any time" and I watched her break down and I almost felt her hug me. She kissed me and rubbed my head and told me she loved me and prayed that I'd be ok. I knew there was only one thing I wanted to do – get better and get back to the country.

I stayed with the vet for two nights. They took really good care of me! Somehow, the veterinarian got me stabilized and let Mom know I would be released! I still could not move and no one knew if I ever would again or not, we just knew I would be happier at home. I would have to take medication for the rest of my life. Some people would be upset about this, but I was just glad I got to go back home to the country.

Mom, Savannah and my Nana stayed with me around the clock for the first few weeks. I felt so bad I could not do anything for myself but I was trying. I had to be spoon-fed and I could not go out to potty on my own.

The girls didn't mind taking care of me. We were all just thankful I was alive. Even my brothers were more tentative and patient with me. We got a stroller so I could go comfortably with them everywhere.

One day, I told my tail to wag and it did! I couldn't believe it! I didn't want it to stop wagging once it started! I wondered what else I could do if I tried hard enough. I tried lifting my head. I got it up a little bit before it fell down. I decided if I woke up the next day and I could still wag my tail, I would try to lift my head again.

I woke up the next morning wondering if wagging my tail was just a dream. I remember lying there and hoping that it was real but being scared to try.

Suddenly Mom's alarm started going off. Breakfast time! I heard Bundy and Hank start to stir in the living room. "Get Up!" I told myself. "Get Up!" I shouted to myself. My shoulders wouldn't move. I sighed in disappointment and waited on Mommy to spoon feed me.

Mom came into the room and my tail started wagging! Breakfast time makes me so excited that my tail started wagging without even trying! Mom cried out in disbelief and swooped me up in a bear hug. We both knew this was a turning point for me.

Later that day, I tried lifting my head to love on Hank and I did it! I couldn't do it for very long that first day but I did it and that's what's important!

Mom came home to find me both lifting my head and wagging my tail! We were all thrilled that I seemed to be making strides to getting better.

Everyday, I tried moving more and more. I got better and better at wagging my tail. Soon I was able to lift my head and keep it up. Next I began trying to roll over on my own. My family had been so good about giving me the care that I needed, but I really wanted to do these things on my own.

The next day we were all lying outside in the sunshine, enjoying the sounds of the birds in the trees. I decided I wanted to roll over on my other side. Mom was on the porch and would've come over instantly to help me but I wanted to do this on my own.

I took a deep breath and as I exhaled I used all my strength and told my paws to roll over. Slowly, my paws and shoulders did what I was telling them to do. The first couple times I toppled back over, but by the third or fourth time I managed to sit up straight and then roll over! Now I was getting somewhere! I could lift myself up and roll over! I looked up to see if Mom had noticed and I wasn't surprised to see her watching me.

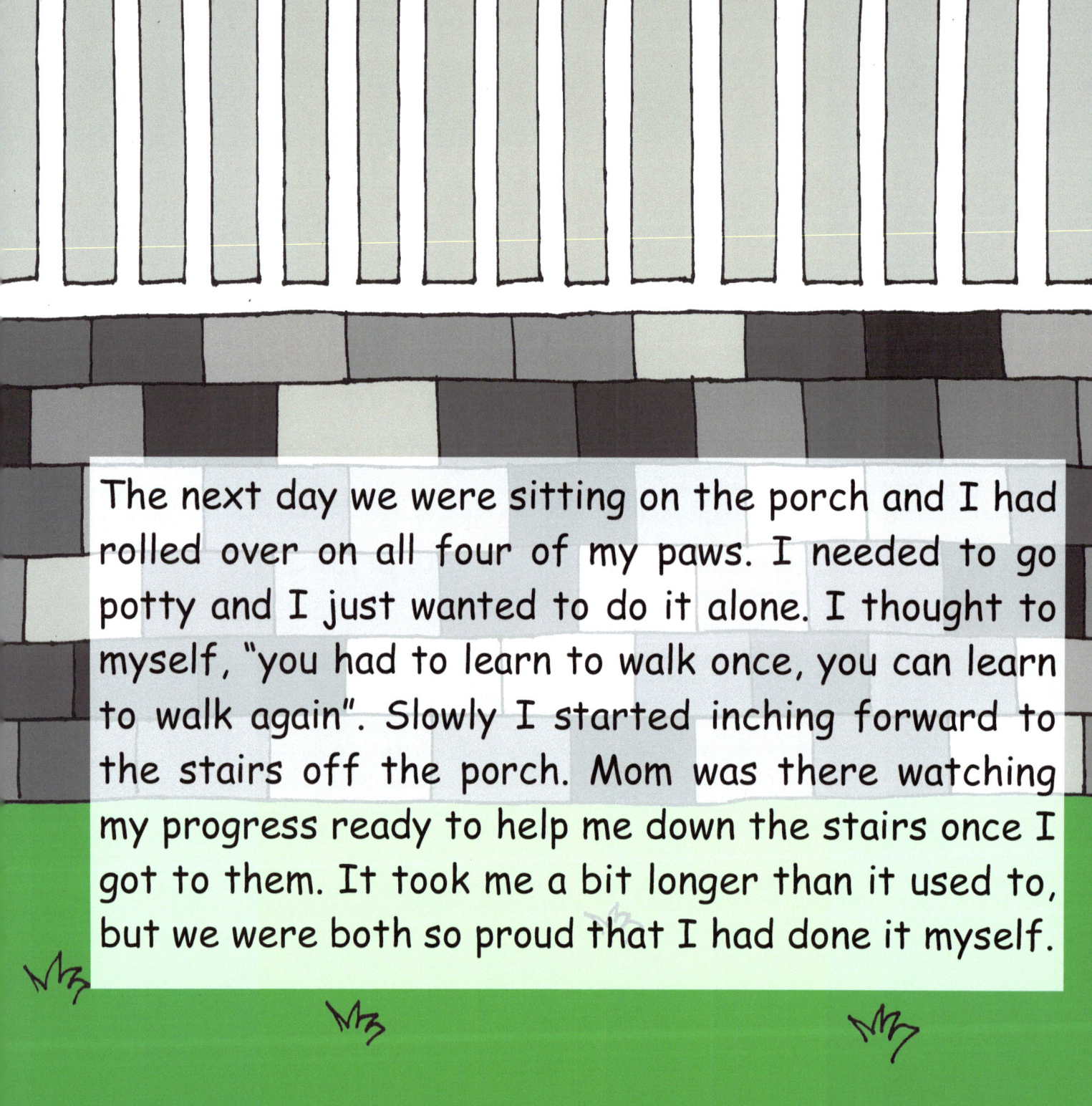

The next day we were sitting on the porch and I had rolled over on all four of my paws. I needed to go potty and I just wanted to do it alone. I thought to myself, "you had to learn to walk once, you can learn to walk again". Slowly I started inching forward to the stairs off the porch. Mom was there watching my progress ready to help me down the stairs once I got to them. It took me a bit longer than it used to, but we were both so proud that I had done it myself.

After learning to crawl, I learned to walk. At first I was slow and stiff. I fell quite a few times, bumping my chin and head. Sometimes my paws would not keep up with my brain, but we all knew I was improving more and more everyday.

One night on our family walk, I decided I wanted out of my stroller. The boys were on leashes and I was not so I quickly got ahead of them. I suddenly realized what I was doing. I was walking, then I was running! I was running again! I hadn't ran in weeks! It felt so good that I could not stop! Mom and Savannah started yelling at me to come back, and I could hear the surprise and joy in their voices. They were happy I was running, but didn't want me getting too far ahead.

Realizing I still needed to mind, I stopped suddenly, turned around and ran as fast as I could back to Mom and Savannah. I only fell a couple times on that short run back, but every time I picked myself back up and ran harder and faster towards my family.

Mom crouched down to pick me up as I leapt in her arms and covered her with kisses. None of us could believe what I had done or was doing. We were all so thankful for the doctor and for believing in each other and in miracles.

Now it is almost five months since I got sick. I have made a 98% complete recovery! The only things different are the medication and a slight wiggle in my walk (which Mom thinks is cute). I continue to thrive in the country with my family and hope on being here many more years. We are all believers in the power of prayer, miracles and hopes.

I hope you enjoyed my "Tail" of Recovery and share it with anyone who might need some inspiration!

See you soon!

www.ingramcontent.com/pod-product-compliance
Lightning Source LLC
Chambersburg PA
CBHW041155290426
44108CB00002B/72